BEST
GRILL
RECIPES
EVER

BEST GRILL RECIPES EVER

FAST AND EASY BARBECUE
PLUS SAUCES, RUBS, AND MARINADES

DANIELLA MALFITANO

THE COUNTRYMAN PRESS

A DIVISION OF W. W. NORTON & COMPANY

INDEPENDENT PUBLISHERS SINCE 1923

Copyright © 2013 by W. W. Norton & Company, Inc.

Previously published as *No Frills Grillin'*

All rights reserved
Printed in the United States of America

For information about permission to reproduce selections from this book, write to
Permissions, The Countryman Press, 500 5th Avenue, New York, NY 10110

For information about special discounts for bulk purchases,
please contact W. W. Norton Special Sales at
specialsales@wwnorton.com or 800-233-4830

Library of Congress Cataloging-in-Publication Data

Names: Malfitano, Daniella, author.
Title: Best Grill Recipes Ever : Fast and Easy Barbecue Plus Sauces, Rubs,
and Marinades / Daniella Malfitano.
Other titles: No frills grillin
Description: Woodstock, VT : The Countryman Press, a division of W. W. Norton
& Company, [2016] | Series: Best ever | Previously published as: No frills grillin'. ?2013. |
Includes index. Identifiers: LCCN 2016010919 | ISBN 9781581573930 (pbk.)
Subjects: LCSH: Barbecuing. | Marinades. | Sauces. | LCGFT: Cookbooks.
Classification: LCC TX840.B3 M325 2013 | DDC 641.7/6—dc23 LC record available at
https://lccn.loc.gov/2016010919

The Countryman Press
www.countrymanpress.com

A division of W. W. Norton & Company, Inc.,
500 Fifth Avenue, New York, NY 10110
www.wwnorton.com

10 9 8 7 6 5 4 3 2 1

TO MY MENTOR AND FRIEND,
"UNCLE" PETER DUMBROWSKI.
THANK YOU FOR BELIEVING IN ME
AND GIVING ME THIS OPPORTUNITY.

BEST GRILL RECIPES EVER
CONTENTS

Introduction

This book will give you all of the inspiration you will need to be a grilling master for the great outdoors or right inside your very own home kitchen! *Best Grill Recipes Ever* contains over 55 irresistible grilling and barbecue recipes that are simple and easy to follow. With recipes ranging from such classic backyard barbecue delights as grilled beef, lamb, pork, chicken, and vegetables to more adventurous dishes, including grilled halibut, shrimp, lobster, corn, and bananas, this grilling book is sure to please. In addition, this wonderful barbecue companion includes recipes for some amazing grilled side dishes and sauces that will aid you in planning the perfect barbecue feast! All of the recipes that I have chosen for this book have been inspired from traditional and unique barbecue favorites. *Best Grill Recipes Ever* will be your perfect backyard and kitchen barbecue companion for preparing exquisite grilled meals. These recipes will inspire you to head to your barbecue or grill pan and get cooking!

With pleasure and an appetite,
Chef Daniella Malfitano

CHAPTER ONE

MEAT ME AT THE GRILL

Grilled Marinated Spareribs

Yield: 4 servings   Prep Time: 25 minutes   Marinating Time: 12 hours
Grilling Time: 2 hours

4½ pounds spareribs

FOR THE MARINADE

2 garlic cloves, pressed

1 small onion, finely chopped

½ cup tomato paste

¼ cup ketchup

⅓ cup honey

¼ cup freshly squeezed orange juice

¼ cup cider vinegar

¼ cup soy sauce

2 tablespoons Worcestershire sauce

1 teaspoon fresh ginger, peeled and grated

1 stalk lemongrass, finely chopped

Freshly ground black pepper

¼ cup finely chopped fresh cilantro, plus more for garnish

Rinse the ribs under cold running water and pat dry with paper towels. Trim away any fat and remove the silver skin from the back of the ribs. Cut the ribs into four portions and place in a nonreactive shallow dish. Set aside.

Marinate the Ribs
In a mixing bowl, combine all the marinade ingredients, stirring to thoroughly blend. Divide the marinade in half, reserving one half for dipping or

drizzling. Generously brush both sides of the ribs with the marinade, reserving the rest of the brushing marinade for basting. Cover and refrigerate the ribs for at least 12 hours, turning the ribs over from time to time.

To Grill

When ready to cook, prepare the grill for indirect grilling. Preheat to medium-high heat. Place the ribs, bone side down, on the hot grill grate, making sure they are not over a direct flame. Grill, covered, at about 325°F for 1½ to 2 hours, or until the meat is tender. Try not to open the grill for the first half hour.

About 20 to 30 minutes before serving, brush with remaining marinade.

Transfer the ribs to a cutting board and let rest for 8 to 10 minutes before cutting into individual or two-rib sections. Transfer the ribs to a serving platter and garnish with fresh cilantro and black pepper to taste. Serve with the reserved marinade that had not been used for basting.

Grilled New York Sirloin Strip Steaks

Yield: 4 servings   **Prep Time: 45 minutes**   **Grilling Time: 18 minutes**

4 boneless strip steaks (8 to 10 ounces each)

4 tablespoons good-quality olive oil

Coarsely ground black pepper

Coarse salt

Bring the steaks to room temperature prior to grilling.

Prepare the grill for direct grilling. Preheat to high heat.

Pat the steaks completely dry with absorbent paper towels. Brush the steaks on both sides with olive oil and season generously with the pepper and salt.

Brush the grill grate with olive oil. Place the steaks on the hot grate and grill for 6 to 9 minutes per side, depending on the thickness of the steak. Test for doneness by inserting an instant-read thermometer into the thickest portion of the meat. The internal temperature should be at least 145°F for medium-rare.

Transfer the steaks to a platter and cover loosely with aluminum foil. Let rest for 3 to 4 minutes before slicing and serving.

Marinated Lamb Shish Kebabs

Yield: 4 servings   **Prep Time: 30 minutes**   **Marinating Time: 12 hours**
Grilling Time: 14 minutes

2 pounds boneless leg of lamb

FOR THE MARINADE

½ teaspoon saffron threads

1 tablespoon warm water

¼ cup freshly squeezed lemon juice

1 tablespoon lemon zest

1 teaspoon coarse salt

Freshly ground black pepper

1 small onion, minced

3 garlic cloves, minced

½ cup plain yogurt

2 bay leaves

TO GRILL

4 tablespoons salted butter

2 tablespoons freshly squeezed lemon juice

8 cherry tomatoes

8 pearl onions, peeled

1 large green bell pepper, seeded and cut into 1-inch squares

1 lemon, cut into wedges, for serving (optional)

Marinate the Lamb

Rinse the lamb under cold running water and pat dry with paper towels. Cut the lamb into 2-inch cubes. Set aside.

Crumble the saffron into a large stainless-steel or glass bowl. Add the warm water and let it sit for at least 5 minutes.

Add the lemon juice, lemon zest, salt, black pepper to taste, onion, and garlic; stir to blend. Add the yogurt, bay leaves, and cubed lamb, tossing well to thoroughly coat the lamb. Cover and refrigerate for at least 4 hours or overnight. The longer you marinate, the better. Stir several times to promote even marinating.

To Grill

Prepare the grill for direct grilling. Preheat to high heat.

Place the butter and lemon juice in a small stainless-steel saucepan. Heat over medium heat until the butter is melted, 1 to 2 minutes. Remove from the heat and set aside.

Thread the marinated lamb and vegetables onto metal skewers. Place the shish kebabs on the hot grate and grill for 2 to 3 minutes per side (8 to 12 minutes total) for medium-rare, or until the lamb reaches your desired doneness. Season with salt and pepper while they grill, and baste with the lemon butter.

Transfer the grilled kebabs to a serving platter. Serve with lemon wedges, if desired.

Grilled T-bone Steaks

Yield: 4 servings   Prep Time: 30 minutes   Grilling Time: 12 minutes

4 T-bone steaks (1-inch thick)

Coarse salt

Coarsely ground black pepper

Pat steaks with a paper towel and then place them on a platter. Season both sides with salt and pepper.

Prepare the grill for direct grilling. Preheat to high heat.

When ready to cook, brush the grill grate with oil. Arrange the steaks on the hot grill grate and grill for 4 to 6 minutes per side for medium-rare (145°F on an instant-read thermometer), or until the steaks reach your desired doneness.

Transfer the steaks to a serving platter or individual plates and allow to rest for about 3 minutes. Season to taste with additional pepper and serve.

Gourmet Burgers

Yield: 4 servings   **Prep Time: 30 minutes**   **Grilling Time: 14 minutes**

1½ pounds ground sirloin, chuck, or round

4 tablespoons herbed butter, sliced

Coarse salt

Freshly ground black pepper

4 hamburger or sandwich rolls

1 tablespoon salted butter, melted

FOR ASSEMBLY

4 slices cheese

Lettuce leaves

Sweet onion, thinly sliced

4 slices ripe tomato

Mayonnaise, mustard, and/or ketchup

Moisten your hands with cold water and divide the ground beef into four equal portions. Form each into a flattened ball and make a well in the center with your thumb.

Place a slice of herbed butter in the center well and cover with the surrounding ground beef, forming a nice, thick patty. Season with salt and pepper.

Cover the burgers with foil and refrigerate until ready to cook.

Prepare the grill for direct grilling. Preheat to high heat.

Place the prepared burgers on the hot grill grate. Grill for 5 to 7 minutes per side for medium, or until an instant-read thermometer inserted through the side of the burger into the center reaches 160°F.

Brush the rolls with melted butter and toast them on the grill for about 45 seconds.

Assemble the Burgers:

Assemble the burgers, top with your favorite condiment and serve.

Tandoori Lamb Chops

Yield: 4 servings   **Prep Time: 20 minutes**   **Marinating Time: 12 hours**
Grilling Time: 10 minutes

8 lamb chops (about 2½ pounds)

FOR THE MARINADE

1 cup Greek yogurt

3 tablespoons freshly squeezed lemon juice

1 (3-inch) piece fresh ginger, peeled and grated

2 garlic cloves, minced

2 tablespoons honey

1 tablespoon garam masala (see tip)

2 teaspoons sweet paprika

2 teaspoons ground cumin

¼ teaspoon freshly grated nutmeg

Pinch of coarse salt

6 thyme sprigs

TO GRILL

Coarse salt

Freshly ground black pepper

Rinse the lamb chops under cold running water and pat dry with paper towels. Using the tip of a sharp knife, make a few slits in each of the lamb chops.

In a large, nonreactive bowl, whisk together the yogurt, lemon juice, ginger, garlic, honey, garam masala, paprika, cumin, nutmeg, and salt until

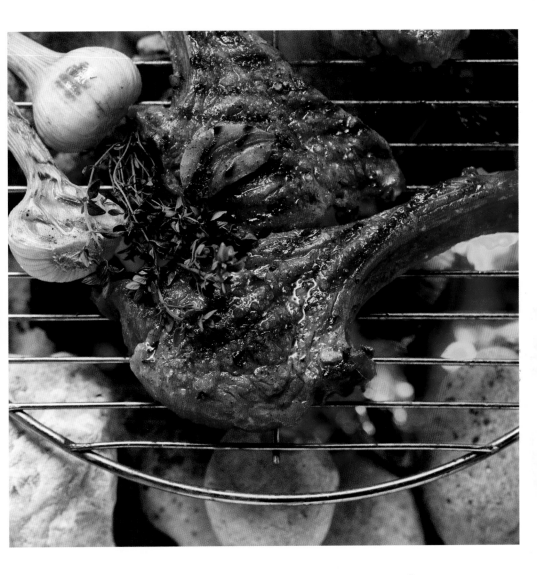

blended. Place the lamb chops in the marinade, turning to completely coat the lamb. Top with the thyme sprigs, cover, and refrigerate overnight.

Prepare the grill for direct grilling. Preheat to medium-high heat. While the grill is heating, remove the lamb from the refrigerator and let stand at room temperature for 30 minutes.

Brush the grill grate with oil. Season the lamb with salt and pepper. Grill to your desired doneness, 4 to 5 minutes per side for medium-rare.

Transfer the lamb to individual plates or a serving platter. Serve.

Tip: Garam masala is a combination of Indian spices and can be found in most supermarkets and specialty markets.

Grilled Filet Mignon

Yield: 4 servings   **Prep Time: 30 minutes**   **Resting Time: 48 minutes**
Grilling Time: 10 minutes

4 slices uncooked bacon (optional)

4 beef tenderloin fillets (1½-inches thick)

Freshly ground black pepper

Coarse salt

Wrap a strip of bacon, if using, around each fillet, securing it with kitchen twine or a wooden toothpick. Season each fillet with pepper and place in a single layer on a platter. Let the beef reach room temperature, about 45 minutes on the kitchen counter.

Prepare the grill for direct grilling. Preheat to high heat.

Prior to placing the fillets on the grill, brush the grill grate with oil. Using tongs, place the fillets on the grill. Let them cook undisturbed for 2 minutes. If flames flare for more than 30 seconds, spray with a little water.

After about 2 minutes, lift the fillets, using tongs, and turn them 90 degrees. Cook for another 3 minutes. Using tongs, gently flip the fillets (one time only) and cook undisturbed for 2 minutes. Again, turn 90 degrees and continue to cook for 3 minutes (for medium-rare).

Check for doneness by pushing on a fillet with your index finger. A rare steak will leave an indentation of your finger. A medium-done steak will give a little, but not leave an indentation. A well-done steak will feel firm to the touch.

Remove the fillets from the grill. Carefully remove the kitchen twine or toothpicks. Transfer to a serving platter and let rest for about 3 minutes. Season to taste with salt and pepper. Serve.

Pork Sausages with Rosemary

Yield: 6 servings **Prep Time: 30 minutes** **Cooking Time: 5 minutes**
Grilling Time: 12 minutes

3 pounds uncooked pork sausages
(sweet or hot Italian, bratwurst, etc.)

1 onion, thinly sliced

3 cups beer

1 cup water

1 tablespoon oil, for brushing

6 rosemary sprigs

Prick each sausage 6 to 8 times with a pin, needle, or slender metal skewer. Arrange the onion slices in the bottom of a skillet or sauté pan just large enough to hold all the sausages. Add the sausages and cover with beer and water. Over medium heat, gradually bring the liquid to a simmer. Cook for 4 to 5 minutes, or until half cooked. Drain the sausages in a colander. When cool enough to handle, separate the sausages into links.

Prepare the grill for direct grilling. Preheat to medium-high heat.

When ready to cook, brush the grill grate with oil. Lightly brush the sausages with oil and place on the prepared grill grate. Grill the sausages for 4 to 6 minutes on each side, or until the casings are nicely browned and crisp.

Brush the rosemary sprigs lightly with oil. Place on the hot grill grate and grill for about 1 minute. Transfer the sausages and rosemary to a platter; let rest for 3 to 4 minutes, then serve.

Rib Eye Steak Tuscan Style

Yield: 2 servings   Prep Time: 20 minutes   Grilling Time: 20 minutes

2 rib eye steaks (1½-inches thick; 10 to 12 ounces each)

Kosher or sea salt

Freshly ground black pepper

2 garlic cloves, finely chopped

1 tablespoon fresh rosemary leaves, chopped

6 fresh sage leaves

½ cup good-quality extra-virgin olive oil

Prepare the grill for direct grilling. Preheat to high heat.

Season the steaks generously with salt and pepper. Brush the grill grate with oil. Place the steaks on the grate and grill until cooked to taste, 7 to 10 minutes per side for rare. Use an instant-read thermometer to check for doneness.

Meanwhile, in a deep dish or serving platter, scatter the garlic, rosemary, and sage leaves over the bottom. Arrange the grilled steak on top of the herbs and pour the olive oil over the steak. Turn several times to completely coat the steak. Spoon the oil that gathers in the bottom of the dish over the steak. Let the steak rest in the marinade for 3 to 5 minutes.

Transfer to plates and serve, spooning the herbed oil over the steak, if desired. Serve with grilled corn and baked potato, if desired.

Sausage & Veggie Skewers

Yield: 4 servings   **Prep Time: 20 minutes**   **Grilling Time: 12 minutes**

1½ pounds sausage (bratwurst or kielbasa work well)

2 red bell peppers, trimmed, seeded, and cut into bite-size pieces

1 medium zucchini, trimmed and cut into rounds

1 small eggplant, trimmed and cut into bite-size pieces

3 tablespoons good-quality olive oil, divided

Salt

Freshly ground black pepper

1 teaspoon dried oregano

Soak 8 wooden skewers in water for 30 minutes. Meanwhile, prepare the grill for direct cooking by preheating to medium-high heat.

Cut the sausage into 1½-inch pieces. In a large bowl, toss the sausage, bell peppers, zucchini, and eggplant with 2 tablespoons of the olive oil; season to taste with salt, black pepper, dried oregano, and additional olive oil.

Thread the sausage and vegetables onto the presoaked skewers, alternating between sliced sausage and vegetables. Grill, turning frequently, until the sausage is browned and cooked through and the vegetables are crisp tender, 10 to 12 minutes, brushing with the remaining olive oil from time to time.

Divide the skewers among plates and serve.

CHAPTER TWO

WINGS & THINGS

Zesty Chicken Wings

Yield: 4 servings   **Prep Time: 30 minutes**   **Marinating Time: 12 hours**
Grilling Time: 15 minutes

FOR THE MARINADE

1 tablespoon olive oil

1 small white onion, finely chopped

2 garlic cloves, finely chopped

½ cup fresh cilantro, finely chopped

2 tablespoons lemon zest

2 tablespoons freshly squeezed lemon juice

2 cups barbecue sauce (your favorite)

¼ cup sherry vinegar

1 teaspoon ground turmeric

FOR THE CHICKEN WINGS

1½ pounds chicken wings

Salt

Freshly ground black pepper

Your favorite dipping sauce (optional)

Prepare the Marinade
Combine all the ingredients for the marinade in a food processor. Pulse until blended well.

Marinate the Chicken Wings
Rinse the chicken wings under cold running water and pat dry with paper towels. Season with salt and pepper.

Place the marinade and chicken wings in a large, resealable plastic freezer bag. Seal the bag securely. Squeeze the bag several times, coating the chicken wings thoroughly with the marinade. Place the bag in the refrigerator and marinate overnight.

To Grill

Prepare the grill for direct grilling. Preheat to medium-high heat. Brush the grill grate lightly with oil. Barbecue the wings over medium-hot coals or at medium-high heat for 5 to 7 minutes on each side (turning once, halfway through) until they are cooked through and golden brown.

Serve with your favorite dipping sauce, if desired.

Grilled Spicy Chicken Halves

**Yield: 2 to 4 servings   Prep Time: 30 minutes   Marinating Time: 4 hours
Grilling Time: 24 minutes**

1 whole chicken (3 to 4 pounds)

FOR THE SPICE RUB

1 tablespoon paprika

1 teaspoon garlic powder

1 teaspoon freshly ground black pepper

½ teaspoon dried thyme, crumbled

½ teaspoon dried oregano, crumbled

½ teaspoon dried rosemary, crumbled

¾ teaspoon salt

Remove any packed giblets in the chicken body cavity. Remove and discard any fat deposits just inside the body and neck cavities. Rinse the chicken inside and out under cold running water, drain, and pat dry with paper towels. Cut the chicken completely in half lengthwise. Set aside.

In a small bowl, combine all of the rub ingredients and stir to mix. Sprinkle the rub on both sides of the chicken. Arrange the chicken in a baking dish, cover, and refrigerate for 1 to 4 hours to allow the spices to penetrate.

When ready to cook, prepare the grill for direct grilling. Preheat to medium. Lightly brush the grill grate with oil. Arrange the chicken halves on the grate with oil. Arrange the chicken halves on the hot grate. Grill, skin side down, directly over medium heat, until grill marks form and the skin starts to turn color. If flare-ups occur move the chicken away from the flames to keep them from burning.

Grill for 10 to 12 minutes. The skin should be golden brown and crisp. Turn the halves over and grill the bone side of the chicken for another 10 to 12 minutes, or until the chicken is cooked through. Reposition the halves occasionally so they cook evenly. For extra flavor, lay fresh rosemary sprigs over the chicken for the last 5 or 10 minutes.

The chicken is done when an instant-read meat thermometer inserted into the thickest part of the thigh reads about 175°F. Juices should run clear. Transfer to a serving platter, let rest for 3 to 5 minutes, and serve.

Chicken Satay with Peanut Sauce

Yield: 6 servings   **Prep Time: 10 minutes**   **Marinating Time: 30 minutes**
Grilling Time: 30 minutes

FOR THE CHICKEN

3 tablespoons honey

4 tablespoons oil

½ teaspoon ground coriander

¼ teaspoon cayenne pepper

4 tablespoons freshly squeezed lemon or lime juice

2 tablespoons soy sauce

2 whole boneless and skinless chicken breasts,
separated into 4 pieces

Freshly ground black pepper

FOR THE PEANUT SAUCE

2 cups coconut milk

1 teaspoon red pepper flakes

½ teaspoon caraway seeds

½ teaspoon ground ginger

½ teaspoon ground coriander

4 garlic cloves, crushed

¼ teaspoon salt

¼ cup peanut butter

¼ cup peanuts, chopped finely, for garnish (optional)

Marinate the Chicken

In a large bowl, stir together the honey, oil, coriander, cayenne, lemon juice, and soy sauce.

Slice the chicken into about 24 (½-inch wide) strips and add to the marinade mixture. Let the chicken sit in the marinade for 30 minutes, or while you prepare the peanut sauce and preheat the grill.

Prepare the Peanut Sauce

While the chicken marinates, prepare the sauce. In a small saucepan, place the coconut milk, red pepper flakes, caraway, ginger, coriander, garlic, and salt and bring to a boil. As soon as it boils, take it off the heat and let sit for 15 minutes.

Stir the peanut butter into the coconut milk mixture and simmer on medium-low heat until the sauce thickens slightly, about 5 minutes or so. Remove from the heat and spoon into a serving bowl; top with chopped peanuts, if using.

To Grill

Soak 6 to 12 wooden skewers (depending on how full you want your skewers to be) for 30 minutes, or have ready metal skewers. Prepare grill for direct cooking. Preheat to high heat. Lightly brush the grill with oil.

Thread the chicken onto the skewers. Season with black pepper. Grill the chicken, 2 to 3 minutes per side. Serve with the peanut dipping sauce.

Marinated BBQ Chicken

Yield: 4 servings   **Prep Time: 10 minutes**   **Marinating Time: 12 hours**
Grilling Time: 20 minutes

2 pounds chicken pieces (drumsticks, thighs, wings, etc.)

FOR THE MARINADE

1 teaspoon salt

2 tablespoons lemon zest

2 tablespoons freshly squeezed lemon juice

8 garlic cloves, finely chopped

½ teaspoon freshly ground black pepper

⅓ cup minced fresh cilantro

1 teaspoon ground turmeric

Sweet chili sauce or your favorite dipping sauce, for serving (optional)

Rinse the chicken under cold running water and pat dry with paper towels.

Marinate the Chicken
Combine all the ingredients for the marinade in a food processor and pulse until well blended.

Place the marinade and chicken pieces in a large, resealable plastic freezer bag. Seal the bag securely. Squeeze the bag several times, until the chicken is thoroughly coated with marinade. Marinate in the refrigerator for 12 hours or overnight.

To Grill

Preheat an outdoor grill to medium-high heat for direct cooking and lightly oil the grate. Barbecue the chicken over medium-hot coals or at medium-high heat for 7 to 10 minutes on each side (turning once, halfway through), until the chicken is cooked through and golden brown.

Serve with sweet chili sauce or your favorite dipping sauce, if desired.

BBQ Chicken Breast with Veggies

Yield: 4 servings   **Prep Time: 15 minutes**   **Marinating Time: 4 hours**
Grilling Time: 30 minutes

4 boneless chicken breast halves

4 ears fresh corn, husked

2 tomatoes, thickly sliced

1 tablespoon olive oil

FOR THE MARINADE

¼ cup freshly squeezed lemon juice

½ cup olive oil

2 garlic cloves, minced

1 small onion, minced

¼ teaspoon ground thyme

¼ teaspoon ground cumin

Kosher or sea salt

Freshly ground black pepper

In a small glass bowl, combine the lemon juice, olive oil, garlic, onion, thyme, cumin, and salt and pepper to taste to create the marinade.

Rinse the chicken under cold running water and pat dry with paper towels.

Place the chicken and the marinade in a large, resealable plastic freezer bag. Seal the bag securely. Squeeze the bag to coat the chicken. Refrigerate for at least 4 hours or up to 24 hours.

Prepare the grill for indirect grilling. Preheat to medium. Grill the chicken over indirect heat for about 8 to 10 minutes on each side, or until a meat thermometer inserted into the center of the breast registers 170°F.

About 10 minutes before the chicken is ready, brush corn and tomatoes with olive oil and season with salt and pepper. Watching carefully, grill for about 5 to 8 minutes until done. Cooking time will depend on grill temperature.

Lemon Garlic
Chicken Kebabs

Yield: 4 servings   **Prep Time: 15 minutes**   **Marinating Time: 1 hour**
Grilling Time: 12 minutes

1½ pounds boneless skinless chicken breasts

2 lemons, cut into wedges

4 oregano or thyme sprigs, for garnish (optional)

FOR THE LEMON–GARLIC MARINADE

3 tablespoons extra-virgin olive oil

2 tablespoons white wine

2 tablespoons freshly squeezed lemon juice

2 tablespoons lemon zest

3 garlic cloves, minced

1 teaspoon dried oregano

1 teaspoon coarse salt

½ teaspoon freshly ground black pepper

Rinse the chicken under cold running water and pat dry with paper towels. Using a sharp knife, cut chicken into 1-inch cubes. Place the chicken in a large, resealable plastic freezer bag.

Marinate the Chicken

In a small bowl, combine the olive oil, white wine, lemon juice, lemon zest, garlic, dried oregano, salt, and pepper, whisking to blend. Pour the marinade into the plastic storage bag with the chicken. Seal bag securely; squeeze the bag several times to thoroughly coat the chicken. Refrigerate for at least one hour.

When ready to cook, prepare the grill for direct grilling. Preheat to high.

Thread chicken cubes onto skewers. Thread lemon wedges onto skewers. Brush the grill grate with oil. Place kebabs on the hot grate and grill until cooked through, 2 to 3 minutes on each side. When done, the chicken will turn white and be firm to the touch.

Transfer the kebabs to a serving platter. Place skewered lemon wedges on the grill and cook for about 1 minute on each side. Serve kebabs garnished with lemon wedges and fresh herbs, if desired.

Grilled Chicken & Pepper Kebabs

Yield: 4 servings   **Prep Time: 20 minutes**   **Marinating Time: 1 hour**
Grilling Time: 10 minutes

2 pounds boneless skinless chicken breasts

FOR THE MARINADE

6 tablespoons freshly squeezed lemon juice

½ cup olive oil

2 teaspoons curry powder

1 tablespoon honey

Salt

Freshly ground black pepper

1 yellow bell pepper, trimmed, seeded, and cut into bite-size pieces

1 red bell pepper, trimmed, seeded, and cut into bite-size pieces

Rinse the chicken under cold running water and pat dry with paper towels. Using a sharp knife, cut the chicken into bite-size cubes. Place the chicken in a large, resealable plastic freezer bag.

Marinate the Chicken
In a small bowl, combine the lemon juice, olive oil, curry powder, honey, salt, and black pepper to taste; whisk to blend. Pour the marinade and prepared bell peppers into the plastic bag with the chicken. Seal the bag securely. Squeeze the bag several times to thoroughly coat the chicken and bell peppers. Refrigerate for at least 1 hour.

To Grill
When ready to cook, prepare the grill for direct grilling. Preheat to high heat. Soak 8 wooden skewers for 30 minutes, or have ready metal skewers.

Thread the chicken and bell peppers onto the skewers, dividing the chicken and bell peppers evenly. Brush the grill grate with oil. Place the kebabs on the hot grate and grill until the chicken is cooked through, 4 to 5 minutes on each side. When done, the chicken should be firm to the touch.

Transfer the kebabs to a serving dish and drizzle with lemon juice, if desired, then serve.

Caribbean Jerk-Glazed Chicken Legs

**Yield: 6 servings   Prep Time: 15 minutes   Marinating Time: 8 hours
Grilling Time: 42 minutes**

6 whole bone-in chicken legs, skin intact

FOR THE MARINADE

½ cup canola oil

½ cup freshly squeezed lime juice

4 tablespoons light brown sugar

2 tablespoons cider vinegar

2 tablespoons dried thyme

2 tablespoons soy sauce

1 tablespoon ground allspice

2 teaspoons ground cinnamon

6 garlic cloves, peeled

6 habanero chiles, stemmed and seeded

8 green onions, roughly chopped

2 shallots, roughly chopped

1 (1-inch) piece fresh ginger, peeled and roughly chopped

Coarse salt

Freshly ground black pepper

Rinse the chicken under cold running water and pat dry with paper towels. Separate the chicken legs from the thighs, using a sharp knife. Place the chicken in a 9 x 13-inch baking dish.

Marinate the Chicken

In the bowl of a food processor, combine all the marinade ingredients, including salt and pepper to taste. Pulse until the mixture is smooth.

Pour the marinade mixture over the chicken. Using clean fingers, massage the marinade into the chicken, making sure to push some up under the skin. Cover the chicken with plastic wrap and refrigerate for at least 8 hours or overnight.

To Grill

Prepare the grill for direct grilling. Preheat to medium-high heat. Brush the grill grate with oil.

Place the chicken on the grill and cook, turning occasionally, until the chicken browns on all sides, 10 to 12 minutes. Transfer the chicken pieces to indirect heat and continue to cook, turning occasionally, until cooked through, about 30 minutes. Transfer the chicken to a serving platter and serve.

Grilled Marinated Chicken Wings with Yogurt Dip

Yield: 6 servings   **Prep Time: 25 minutes**   **Marinating Time: 8 hours**
Grilling Time: 20 minutes

2 pounds chicken wings, skin intact

3 limes, halved

1 tablespoon honey

FOR THE MARINADE

½ cup canola oil

½ cup freshly squeezed lime juice

4 tablespoons light brown sugar

2 tablespoons cider vinegar

2 tablespoons dried thyme

2 tablespoons soy sauce

1 tablespoon ground allspice

2 teaspoons ground cinnamon

6 garlic cloves, peeled

2 shallots, roughly chopped

1 (1-inch) piece fresh ginger, peeled and roughly chopped

Coarse salt

Freshly ground black pepper

FOR THE HONEY–LIME YOGURT DIP

1 cup plain yogurt

2 tablespoons honey

1 teaspoon lime zest

Rinse the chicken under cold running water and pat dry with paper towels. Place the chicken wings in a 9 x 13-inch baking dish.

Marinate the Chicken

In the bowl of a food processor, combine all the marinade ingredients, including salt and pepper to taste. Pulse until the mixture is smooth.

Pour the marinade mixture over the chicken. With clean hands, massage the marinade into the chicken. Cover the chicken with plastic wrap and refrigerate for at least 8 hours or overnight.

Prepare the grill for direct grilling. Preheat to medium-high heat.

Prepare the Yogurt Dip

In a small bowl, combine the yogurt, honey, and lime zest and stir until well blended. Chill until ready to serve.

To Grill

Brush the grill grate with oil. Place the chicken on the hot grill grate. Grill until the wings are golden brown and crisp on the outside and cooked through, 8 to 10 minutes per side.

Brush the lime halves with the honey and grill until golden and fragrant, 45 to 60 seconds. Transfer the chicken and limes to a serving platter. Serve with the Yogurt Dip.

CHAPTER THREE

WALK THE PLANK

Cedar Plank Salmon with Herb Dressing

Yield: 4 servings   Prep Time: 20 minutes   Soaking Time: 1 hour
Grilling Time: 25 minutes

4 wild Alaskan salmon fillets (6 ounces each)

2 green onions, trimmed and finely chopped

3 shallots, peeled and thinly sliced

3 dill sprigs, finely chopped

Juice of 2 limes

2 tablespoons good-quality olive oil

2 tablespoons red wine vinegar

Coarse salt

Freshly ground black pepper

Immerse and soak a cedar plank in salted water for at least 1 hour or overnight; drain and wipe away any excess water.

Prepare the grill for indirect grilling. Preheat to medium-high.

Rinse the salmon fillets under cold running water and pat completely dry with paper towels.

In a glass bowl, combine the green onions, shallots, dill, lime juice, olive oil, and red wine vinegar. Season to taste with salt and pepper. Spoon the mixture over the top of the salmon.

Place the cedar plank in the center of the prepared grill grate, away from the heat. Cover for 4 to 5 minutes, until the plank starts to smoke. Place the salmon fillets on the prepared cedar plank. Cover and cook for 15 to 25 minutes, or until the salmon flakes easily or until the desired degree of doneness is achieved. Check the plank occasionally and mist with water if the edges start to catch fire. The grilling time will vary, depending on the thickness of the salmon. Serve.

BBQ Sea Bass

Yield: 4 servings   Prep Time: 30 minutes   Grilling Time: 20 minutes

2 prepared sea bass (about 1½ pounds each)

8 fresh kaffir lime leaves, cut in half lengthwise

8 fresh bay leaves, cut in half lengthwise, plus more for garnish

3 tablespoons olive oil, for brushing

Coarse salt

Freshly ground black pepper

Lemon wedges, for garnish

Prepare the grill for direct grilling. Preheat to medium-low heat.

Using a sharp knife, gently cut into the fish, making 8 diagonal cuts on each side. Place a lime leaf half and bay leaf half into each slit.

Brush the fish all over with olive oil and season with salt and pepper. Using a fish basket, grill for 8 to 10 minutes on each side, turning occasionally.

Transfer to a serving platter. Drizzle with any remaining olive oil. Adjust the seasoning, if necessary. Garnish with lemon wedges and the remaining bay leaves. Serve.

Salmon Kebabs with Spicy Marinade

Yield: 4 servings   **Prep Time: 20 minutes**   **Marinating Time: 30 minutes**
Grilling Time: 8 minutes

1 pound salmon fillet, skin removed

FOR THE MARINADE

2 tablespoons olive oil

1 tablespoon freshly squeezed orange juice

¼ cup honey

1 tablespoon rice vinegar

1 teaspoon fennel seeds

1 (½-inch) piece fresh ginger, peeled and grated

1 garlic clove, minced

1 small onion, cut into strips

4 to 5 strips fresh orange peels

Freshly ground black pepper

Soak 4 to 8 (depending on how full you want your skewers to be) wooden skewers in water for 30 minutes, or have ready metal skewers.

Meanwhile, rinse the salmon under cold running water and pat completely dry with paper towels. Remove any bones. Using a sharp knife, slice the salmon into bite-size pieces. Thread the salmon onto skewers and place in a shallow dish.

In a small bowl, whisk together the olive oil, orange juice, honey, rice vinegar, fennel seeds, ginger, garlic, onion, and orange peels. Season to taste with pepper. Pour the mixture over the salmon, turning to coat. Let stand at room temperature for 30 minutes. Transfer the marinade to a small saucepan and simmer on medium-low heat for several minutes.

Prepare the grill for direct grilling. Preheat to medium-high heat.

Lightly oil the grill grate. Place the salmon skewers on the preheated grill and cook for 4 minutes per side, brushing frequently with marinade, or until the fish flakes easily with a fork.

Transfer to a serving platter or individual plates, drizzle with the simmered marinade, and serve.

Swordfish with Olive Tapenade on Saffron Risotto

Yield: 4 servings   **Prep Time: 25 minutes**   **Cooking Time: 25 minutes**
Grilling Time: 10 minutes

FOR THE SAFFRON RISOTTO

4½ cups chicken stock, divided

¼ cup (½ stick) salted butter, divided

½ onion, finely chopped (about ½ cup)

1½ cups Arborio rice, toasted

½ cup dry white wine

½ teaspoon saffron strands, chopped and dissolved in
    ½ cup hot chicken stock

⅓ cup freshly grated Parmesan cheese

Coarse salt

Freshly ground black pepper

FOR THE TAPENADE

2 cups pitted black olives (two 6-ounce cans or
    1½ cups pitted kalamata olives, rinsed and drained)

2 anchovy fillets, rinsed

1 garlic clove, coarsely chopped

2 tablespoons capers, drained

1 tablespoon Dijon mustard

1 tablespoon fresh basil leaves

Freshly ground black pepper

1 tablespoon freshly squeezed lemon juice

2 tablespoons extra-virgin olive oil

1 teaspoon red pepper flakes

FOR THE SWORDFISH

4 swordfish steaks (1-inch thick, 6 to 8 ounces each)

2 tablespoons olive oil

Coarse salt

Freshly ground black pepper

12 cherry tomatoes, trimmed and halved

Fresh basil or oregano, for garnish

Note: Toast the Arborio rice in a clean, dry pan over medium heat for 3 to 5 minutes, or until the rice looks slightly browned and smells a bit toasted.

Prepare the Saffron Risotto

In a medium saucepan over medium-high heat, bring the chicken stock to a simmer. Maintain a slow simmer while making the risotto.

In a heavy, 4-quart pot over medium heat, melt 3 tablespoons of the butter; add the onion and sauté until the onion is soft but not browned, 1 to 2 minutes. Add the toasted rice and stir with a wooden spoon for 2 to 3 minutes, coating all the grains. Add the wine; stirring continuously until all the liquid is completely absorbed.

Add the hot chicken stock ½ cup at a time, stirring frequently until all the liquid is absorbed. Run the wooden spoon across the bottom of the pot to make sure all the liquid is absorbed before adding the next ½ cup. Reserve about ¼ cup of stock to add at the end.

When the rice has cooked for about 15 minutes, add half of the dissolved saffron and its stock. Continue to stir; when all the liquid has been absorbed, add the remaining saffron and its stock.

After about 18 minutes, when the rice is tender but firm, add the reserved ¼ cup of hot chicken stock and stir until the liquid is absorbed. Remove the pot from the heat and add the remaining tablespoon of butter and the Parmesan cheese, stirring to combine. Season with salt and black pepper to taste.

Transfer to warmed plates and serve immediately with the grilled swordfish and tapenade.

Prepare the Tapenade

While the risotto cooks, place all the tapenade ingredients in the bowl of a food processor. Process to combine, stopping to scrape down the sides of the bowl. Pulse until the mixture becomes a coarse paste, about 1½ minutes total. Transfer to a small bowl and set aside until ready to use.

Prepare the Swordfish

Meanwhile, prepare the grill for direct grilling. Preheat to high heat.

Rinse the swordfish under cold running water and pat dry with paper towels. Brush both sides of the fillets with olive oil and season with salt and black pepper.

Place the seasoned swordfish in a fish basket or on a fish grate and place on the hot grill grate. Grill for 4 to 5 minutes on each side, or until cooked through.

Place the fish on top of the prepared risotto. Garnish with a generous spoonful of tapenade, the cherry tomato halves, and sprigs of fresh oregano or basil and serve.

Monkfish and Scallop Kebabs

Yield: 4 servings   **Prep Time: 30 minutes**   **Marinating Time: 15 minutes**
Grilling Time: 6 minutes

1 pound monkfish, trimmed and cut into 1-inch cubes

1 pound scallops, tough tendons removed

Leaves from 2 sprigs rosemary

1 garlic clove, finely chopped

6 tablespoons good-quality olive oil

12 cherry tomatoes

1 onion, cut into pieces

Coarse salt

Freshly ground black pepper

Freshly squeezed lemon juice, for serving

Soak 8 wooden skewers in water for 30 minutes, or have ready metal skewers.

Place the monkfish and scallops in a large bowl.

Chop the rosemary leaves very finely. Place the rosemary and chopped garlic in a small bowl and add the olive oil, mixing to combine. Pour the oil mixture over the monkfish and scallops, gently tossing to thoroughly coat. Let marinate for 15 minutes.

Prepare the grill for direct grilling. Preheat to medium-high heat.

Thread the skewers with the fish, scallops, and vegetables. Season the kebabs with salt and pepper. Arrange the kebabs on a hot grate and grill for 2 to 3 minutes on all sides, or until the fish is white and cooked through.

Transfer the kebabs to a serving platter. Drizzle with lemon juice and serve.

BBQ Shrimp with Garlic Mayonnaise

Yield: 4 servings **Prep Time: 30 minutes** **Marinating Time: 30 minutes** **Grilling Time: 4 minutes**

FOR THE GARLIC MAYONNAISE

½ cup mayonnaise

2 garlic cloves, minced

FOR THE MARINATED SHRIMP

3 garlic cloves, chopped

2 teaspoons fresh ginger, peeled and grated

½ cup teriyaki sauce

1 cup Clamato juice, or a 1:1 mixture clam juice and tomato juice

1 tablespoon freshly squeezed lemon juice

1½ pounds extra-large shrimp, shell and tail intact

Lemon slices, for garnish

Your favorite crusty bread, for serving

Prepare the Garlic Mayonnaise
Combine the mayonnaise and garlic in a small bowl. Cover and refrigerate until ready to use.

Prepare the Marinated Shrimp
In a small bowl, combine the garlic, ginger, teriyaki sauce, Clamato juice or equivalent, and lemon juice. Set aside.

Using scissors, cut each shrimp shell and devein the shrimp, leaving the shell on. Place the shrimp in a large bowl and pour the marinade over the shrimp. Gently toss to coat. Marinate for 20 to 30 minutes (no longer) prior to grilling.

While the shrimp is marinating, prepare the grill for direct grilling. Preheat to medium-high heat.

Place the shrimp on a fish grate. Grill for about 2 minutes on each side, or until the shells are hot pink and the shrimp is opaque.

Transfer to individual plates. Serve with the lemon slices, the Garlic Mayonnaise, and your favorite crusty bread.

Grilled Halibut

Yield: 4 servings   Prep Time: 30 minutes   Marinating Time: 30 minutes
Grilling Time: 12 minutes

4 halibut fillets (6 to 8 ounces each)

1 tablespoon vegetable oil, for brushing

2 lemons, sliced

FOR THE MARINADE

4 garlic cloves, chopped

1 tablespoon fresh ginger, peeled and grated

2 tablespoons fresh cilantro, minced

3 tablespoons sugar

¼ cup Asian fish sauce

3 tablespoons sesame oil

3 tablespoons rice vinegar

Coarse salt

Freshly ground black pepper

Rinse the fish under cold running water and pat dry with paper towels. Arrange the fish in a glass baking dish just large enough to hold them.

Prepare the Marinade
Using a mortar and pestle, pound the garlic, ginger, cilantro, and sugar until a paste forms. Work in the fish sauce, sesame oil, vinegar, salt, and pepper to taste. Spoon the marinade onto both sides of the fish fillets. Cover the fish with plastic wrap and marinate in the refrigerator for 30 minutes, turning once.

Grill the Fish
Meanwhile, prepare the grill for direct grilling. Preheat to high heat.

When ready to cook, brush the fillets lightly with oil. Place the fish on the hot grill grate and grill until each side is charred and cooked through, 4 to 6 minutes per side. Drizzle with lemon juice while the fish is cooking.

Transfer to a serving platter and serve immediately with lemon slices.

Grilled Lobster with Butter & Lemons

Yield: 4 servings   Prep Time: 15 minutes   Grilling Time: 14 minutes

4 fresh live lobsters (1½ pounds each)

1 cup (2 sticks or 8 ounces) salted butter, melted

Coarse salt

Freshly ground black pepper

2 lemons, halved

Prepare the grill for direct grilling. Preheat to high heat.

To kill the lobster prior to grilling, position the tip of your knife in the center of the lobster's head. Plunge the knife blade between the lobster's eyes. This method kills the lobster instantly and humanely. Cut the lobster in half lengthwise, starting at the head and working your way down to the tail.

Remove and discard the papery sac from the head of the lobster. Remove the vein running the length of the tail. Remove the claws, collecting any lobster juices in a small bowl.

When ready to cook, brush oil on the grill grate. Place the lobster claws on the hot grill and cover. Grill for about 3 minutes. Brush the cut side of the lobster with butter and season with salt and pepper. Place the lobster, cut side down, on the grill; cook for about 3 minutes. Turn over and brush with any reserved juices. Grill, cut side up, for 6 to 8 minutes, or until the flesh is white, firm, and just cooked, brushing with butter several times. Do not overcook. The claws should take 12 to 14 minutes; and the body and tail, 8 to 10 minutes total.

Place the lemon halves on the grill for 1 minute or so. Transfer the lobster to a serving platter and serve with remaining melted butter and lemons.

Scallops in the Half Shell with Garlic Butter

Yield: 12 pieces   **Prep Time: 20 minutes**   **Grilling Time: 5 minutes**

12 large scallops with coral, in the shell (see tip)

½ cup (1 stick) salted butter, at room temperature

3 garlic cloves, pressed

½ tablespoon fresh parsley, finely chopped

Salt

Freshly ground black pepper

Prepare the grill for direct grilling. Preheat to medium-high heat.

Scrub the scallop shells with a hard kitchen brush. Use a thin, dull knife to cut open each shell. Rinse to remove all the sand and grit and discard all the contents except the large white muscle and the coral roe connected to it. Pat dry.

In a medium skillet, melt the butter and add the pressed garlic. Sauté on low heat until the garlic is fragrant; do not burn. Add the parsley to the garlic-butter mixture. Spoon the garlic butter into the scallop shells, dividing equally among the shells. Season lightly with salt and pepper.

Place the scallops on the hot grill grate and cook for 3 to 5 minutes. The scallops are done as soon as they turn white and are no longer translucent. Do not overcook or the scallops will lose their flavor and become tough. Serve immediately.

Tip: Select fresh creamy pink, white, or orange scallops with a sweet odor.

Grilled Tuna, Avocado, & Lemon

Yield: 4 servings   **Prep Time: 25 minutes**   **Marinating Time: 5 minutes**
Grilling Time: 10 minutes

4 tuna steaks (1-inch thick; 5 ounces each)

3½ tablespoons good-quality olive oil, divided

Kosher salt

1 teaspoon freshly squeezed lemon juice

1 garlic clove, minced

Freshly ground black pepper

½ teaspoon fresh oregano, finely chopped

Pinch of crushed red pepper flakes

1 tablespoon fresh basil, finely chopped

2 ripe avocados, halved and pitted

2 lemons, halved

4 fresh basil leaves, for garnish

FOR THE TOMATOES AND OLIVES

1 tablespoons olive oil, divided

2 garlic cloves, minced

1 large ripe tomato, trimmed and finely diced

Pinch of dried thyme

Salt

3 tablespoons black olives, pitted and chopped

Prepare the grill for direct grilling. Preheat to medium-high heat.

Pat the tuna steaks with paper towels to remove any excess moisture and then place them in a shallow baking dish.

In a small bowl, combine 2 tablespoons of the oil, salt to taste, and the lemon juice, garlic, black pepper, oregano, red pepper flakes, and basil. Set aside for 5 minutes to let the flavors infuse.

Brush the marinade on both sides of the tuna and let stand for 5 minutes.

Brush the grill grate with oil. Grill the steaks on the preheated grill for 2 to 5 minutes on each side, or until they reach your desired doneness. For the best flavor, the tuna should still be pink in the center.

Just prior to removing the tuna from the grill, brush the halved avocados and lemons lightly with the remaining 1½ tablespoons of oil and grill for about 1 minute.

Prepare the Tomatoes and Olives:
Meanwhile, in a medium saucepan, heat 1 tablespoon of the oil over medium-high heat. Add the garlic and sauté, stirring, until fragrant, about 45 seconds. Stir in the diced tomato, thyme, and salt to taste. Bring to a simmer, lower the heat, and cook until slightly thickened, 5 to 7 minutes. Stir in the olives.

To Assemble:
Arrange the grilled tuna steaks, avocado halves, and lemon halves on individual plates. Place a basil leaf on top of each tuna steak and top with the tomato mixture. Serve.

CHAPTER FOUR

GREEN YOUR GRILL

Grilled Green Asparagus

Yield: 4 servings   **Prep Time: 15 minutes**   **Grilling Time: 10 minutes**

1 pound fresh asparagus, trimmed

2 tablespoons olive oil

1 garlic clove, minced

1 tablespoon freshly squeezed lemon juice

Freshly ground black pepper

Prepare the grill for direct grilling. Preheat to medium-high heat.

Lay the trimmed asparagus in a shallow baking dish.

In a small bowl, combine the oil, garlic, lemon juice, and pepper, whisking to mix. Gently brush both sides of the asparagus with the mixture. Place the asparagus on the hot grill grate and cook until lightly browned and crisp tender, 3 to 5 minutes per side depending on thickness of asparagus. Drizzle with any remaining marinade and serve.

Summer Veggies

Yield: 4 servings   **Prep Time: 30 minutes**   **Grilling Time: 16 minutes**

2 medium eggplants, cut crosswise into ½-inch slices

Coarse salt

½ cup cold-pressed olive oil

2 to 3 tablespoons freshly squeezed lemon juice

2 teaspoons lemon zest

2 garlic cloves, finely chopped

Freshly ground black pepper

1 large red bell pepper, seeded and cut into thick strips

1 large yellow bell pepper, seeded and cut into thick strips

4 green peppers, left whole

2 garlic bulbs, papery skins removed and discarded, cut in half

1 loaf crusty bread, sliced and grilled (optional)

Arrange the sliced eggplant in a single layer on a large rack placed over a baking sheet. Sprinkle both sides of the eggplant generously with coarse salt. Let stand for 20 to 30 minutes; this will draw the bitter juices from the eggplant. Rinse the eggplant under cold water and pat dry with paper towels.

Meanwhile, prepare the grill for direct grilling. Preheat to high heat.

In a small bowl, mix the olive oil, lemon juice and zest, chopped garlic, salt, and black pepper to taste. Arrange the eggplant, bell and green peppers, and garlic halves on a preheated vegetable grate or preheated grill basket, brush lightly with the oil mixture, and place on the hot grill grate.

Grill for 4 to 8 minutes per side, or until nicely browned on all sides. Transfer the grilled vegetables to a serving platter and drizzle with the remaining oil mixture.

Serve warm or cold with crusty bread, if desired.

Grilled Red Spring Onions & Herbs

Yield: 4 servings   **Prep Time: 15 minutes**   **Grilling Time: 7 minutes**

2 bunches red spring onions, trimmed

Good-quality olive oil, for brushing

Salt

Freshly ground black pepper

2 to 3 rosemary sprigs

4 to 6 fresh lemon leaves

Juice of 1 lemon, for drizzling (see tip)

Prepare the grill for indirect grilling. Preheat to medium-low heat.

Brush each spring onion with olive oil and season to taste with salt and pepper. Place the onions on the grill and cook for 3 to 4 minutes, depending on the size of the onions, until lightly charred. Turn and grill for 2 to 3 additional minutes, or until the onion bulbs are softened. Brush the rosemary and lemon leaves with olive oil and grill for 45 to 60 seconds, or until fragrant.

Transfer the onions and herbs to a plate or platter. Drizzle with freshly squeezed lemon juice and season to taste with additional salt and pepper. Serve.

Tip: You may replace the lemon juice with balsamic vinegar, if desired.

Sweet Corn on the Cob

Yield: 4 servings   Prep Time: 20 minutes   Grilling Time: 10 minutes

½ cup (1 stick or 4 ounces) salted butter, at room temperature, plus more for serving

1 garlic clove, minced

8 ears sweet corn, husked

Coarse salt

Prepare the grill for direct grilling. Preheat to high heat.

In a small bowl, whisk the ½ cup of butter and garlic together until creamy and smooth.

When ready to cook, lightly brush each ear of corn with the garlic butter and arrange on the hot grill grate.

Grill the corn until the kernels are browned on all sides, 8 to 10 minutes total, turning as necessary and brushing with the remaining garlic butter.

Transfer from the grill to a serving tray or individual plates. Season with butter and salt to taste. Serve immediately.

Portobello Mushrooms

Yield: 4 servings   Prep Time: 10 minutes   Marinating Time: 30 minutes Grilling Time: 10 minutes

4 large portobello mushrooms

2 garlic cloves, cut into slivers

5 rosemary sprigs, 1 stripped of its leaves

½ cup plus 2 tablespoons balsamic vinegar, divided

Kosher salt

Freshly ground black pepper

1 cup extra-virgin olive oil

Trim the stems from the mushrooms. Wipe the caps clean with a moist paper towel or mushroom brush.

Place the mushrooms on a cutting board, gill side up. With a sharp knife, make a series of slits in the portobellos, and insert the garlic slivers and rosemary leaves.

In a nonreactive bowl, combine ½ cup of the vinegar and salt and pepper to taste and whisk to blend. Whisk in the oil. Pour some of the mixture into the bottom of a baking dish and arrange the portobellos in it, gill side up.

Gently swish the mushrooms around to coat with the marinade. Spoon the remaining mixture over the mushrooms. Refrigerate, covered, for at least 30 minutes, or up to 3 hours.

Prepare the grill for direct grilling. Preheat to high heat.

Remove the mushrooms from the marinade. Whisk the remaining 2 tablespoons of balsamic vinegar into the marinade. Arrange the mushroom caps on the hot grate, gill side down. Grill for 3 minutes, turn the mushrooms over, and spoon on some marinade. Continue to grill until the caps are tender and browned, 5 to 6 minutes.

Transfer to a platter or plates and garnish with the four remaining rosemary sprigs. Serve immediately.

Marinated Veggie Kebabs

Yield: 4 servings   Prep Time: 30 minutes   Grilling Time: 10 minutes

FOR THE MARINADE

2 garlic cloves, finely chopped

2 tablespoons balsamic vinegar

½ cup good-quality olive oil

2 thyme sprigs, finely chopped

2 oregano sprigs, finely chopped

1 rosemary sprig, finely chopped

Coarse salt

Freshly ground black pepper

FOR THE KEBABS

3 small zucchinis, peeled in strips and thickly sliced

2 ears fresh corn, husked and thickly sliced

1 red bell pepper, cut into bite-size pieces

1 yellow bell pepper, cut into bite-size pieces

1 green bell pepper, cut into bite-size pieces

4 sweet onions, cut into quarters

4 rosemary sprigs

Prepare the Marinade

Soak 8 wooden skewers in water for 30 minutes. Meanwhile, in a small bowl, mix together the garlic, vinegar, oil, herbs, and salt and black pepper to taste. Set aside.

Prepare the Kebabs

Prepare the grill for direct grilling. Preheat to medium-high heat.

Skewer the vegetables and rosemary sprigs onto the presoaked wooden skewers and brush generously with marinade. Arrange the skewers on a vegetable grate or directly on the hot grill grate. Brushing with the marinade occasionally and turning for even cooking, grill 8 to 10 minutes, then serve.

Banana Leaves Stuffed with Rice & Veggies

Yield: 4 servings   **Prep Time: 35 minutes**   **Cooking Time: 25 minutes**
Grilling Time: 12 minutes

½ cup uncooked basmati rice

1 to 2 whole banana leaves

2 tablespoons canola oil

1 (1½-inch) piece fresh ginger, peeled and finely chopped

1 garlic clove, finely chopped

¼ cup bean sprouts

1 bunch green onions, sliced into rings

1 red bell pepper, seeded and finely chopped

½ cup fresh mango, peeled, pitted, and finely chopped

¼ cup unsalted peanuts, coarsely chopped

4 cilantro sprigs, finely chopped

½ cup sweet chili pepper sauce, divided

Soak 16 wooden toothpicks in water for 30 minutes.

Meanwhile, rinse the rice in a colander under cold running water. In a medium pot, bring 1½ cups of water to a boil and add the rice. Cover and cook over low heat for 5 to 20 minutes, or until the water is absorbed and the rice is light and fluffy.

Using scissors, cut the banana leaves into 8 pieces, each about 8 by 10 inches. In a large pot, blanch the leaves in boiling water for about 45 seconds, then plunge into ice-cold water to stop the cooking process. This makes the leaves soft and pliable.

Heat the oil in a wok or skillet. Add the ginger and garlic; stir-fry for 1 to 2

minutes, until fragrant. Add the bean sprouts, green onions, and bell pepper; stir-fry for 2 to 3 minutes, stirring constantly.

Add the stir-fried mixture to the rice along with the chopped mango, peanuts, and cilantro. Drizzle sweet chili pepper sauce to taste into the rice mixture, reserving the remaining sauce for dipping.

Lay a piece of banana leaf on a cutting board or mat, dark side down. Place a scoop of prepared rice mixture in the center of the leaf and fold over the sides. Fold over the top and bottom ends of the banana leaf to enclose the rice mixture. Secure each end with a presoaked wooden toothpick. Repeat the process for remaining seven pieces.

When ready to cook, prepare the grill for direct grilling. Preheat to high heat.

Brush each banana leaf packet with oil and place on the hot grill grate and grill until the banana leaves are browned and the rice mixture is heated through, 3 to 6 minutes per side. Transfer to a serving platter. Remove the toothpicks, slice, and serve with sweet chili pepper dipping sauce.

Grilled Beets with Wilted Greens

Yield: 4 servings   **Prep Time: 20 minutes**   **Grilling Time: 55 minutes**
Resting Time: 10 minutes

6 medium beets, greens attached

Good-quality olive oil, plus more for beet greens and drizzling

Salt

Freshly ground black pepper

2 thyme sprigs

2 teaspoons salted butter

Prepare the grill for indirect cooking. Preheat to medium-high heat.

Remove the greens from the beets and set aside. Scrub the beets and trim the ends. In 2 batches of 3 beets each, place the beets on a sheet of aluminum foil. Drizzle each batch with olive oil and season to taste with salt and pepper. Add a sprig of thyme to each foil packet, cover the beets with foil, and crimp the edges to secure.

Cook the beets in their foil packets, on indirect heat with the lid closed, for 45 to 55 minutes. To check for doneness, pierce with a skewer or the tines of a fork.

Remove the foil packets from the grill, and let rest for about 10 minutes.

Meanwhile, rinse the beet greens and shake to dry. Heat a splash of olive oil and the butter in a skillet. Sauté the beet greens on medium-high heat until just wilted.

Carefully open the foil and peel the skin off the beets, using paper towels. Cut the beets into wedges and divide the beets and greens among four plates. Drizzle with olive oil and season to taste with pepper, then serve immediately.

Grilled Marinated Tofu & Veggies

Yield: 4 servings   **Prep Time:** 20 minutes   **Marinating Time:** 3 hours
Grilling Time: 8 minutes

1 pound extra-firm tofu, well pressed

½ cup low-sodium tamari soy sauce

¼ cup rice vinegar

1 tablespoon fresh ginger, peeled and finely chopped

1 tablespoon toasted sesame oil

1 garlic clove, finely chopped

4 thyme sprigs, plus more for garnish

1 bunch green onions, trimmed to 3- to 4-inch lengths
    for threading onto skewers

1 red bell pepper, seeded and cut into bite-size pieces

8 button mushrooms, cleaned

Paprika, for sprinkling as a garnish

Cut the pressed tofu into 1½-inch cubes and place in a shallow dish.

In a small bowl, combine the tamari, rice vinegar, ginger, sesame oil, and garlic. Pour the mixture over the tofu and stir to thoroughly coat. Refrigerate and marinate at least 3 hours, or overnight.

Soak 4 to 8 wooden skewers in water for 30 minutes, or have ready metal skewers. Meanwhile, prepare the grill for direct grilling. Preheat to medium-high heat.

Remove the tofu from the marinade and drain well, reserving the marinade. Toss the green onion, bell pepper, and mushrooms in the reserved marinade. Thread the tofu and vegetables onto the skewers. Brush the kebabs with any remaining marinade.

Brush the grill grate with oil. Grill the kebabs for 3 to 4 minutes on each

side, or until the tofu is golden brown and the vegetables are tender. Sprinkle with paprika to garnish.

CHAPTER FIVE

GET SAUCED
ON THE SIDE

BBQ Sauce

Yield: 4 servings   **Prep Time: 15 minutes**   **Cooking Time: 12 minutes**

1 tablespoon vegetable oil

2 garlic cloves, finely chopped

2 red chili peppers, finely chopped

1 (10.75-ounce) can tomato purée

3 tablespoons ketchup

¼ cup vegetable stock

Salt

Freshly ground black pepper

½ teaspoon celery seeds

1 teaspoon sweet paprika

½ teaspoon dry mustard

Worcestershire sauce

Tabasco sauce

In a saucepan, heat the oil over medium heat. Sauté the garlic and chili peppers until soft, tender, and fragrant. Add the tomato purée, ketchup, and vegetable stock. Season with salt and black pepper to taste and add the celery seeds, paprika, and dry mustard. Bring to a boil, then lower the heat and simmer for 10 to 12 minutes.

Stir in the Worcestershire and Tabasco sauce to taste; let cool. Brush on grilled meats or spare ribs.

Chili-Orange Marinade

Yield: 1 cup marinade   Prep Time: 20 minutes

¼ cup rice vinegar

¼ cup low-sodium soy sauce

¼ cup freshly squeezed orange juice

1½ tablespoons chili oil

2 tablespoons fresh ginger, peeled and chopped

4 small dried red chili peppers, finely chopped

3 garlic cloves, sliced

In a small bowl, whisk together the vinegar, soy sauce, orange juice, chili oil, ginger, chili peppers, and garlic.

Use the mixture to marinate meat at room temperature for 30 minutes or in the refrigerator for up to 2 hours.

Tip: The yield is enough to marinate about 3 pounds of meat. Discard the used marinade after each use.

Gorgonzola Dip with Breadsticks

Yield: 4 servings   **Prep Time: 10 minutes**

3½ ounces Gorgonzola cheese, cubed

¼ cup heavy cream

⅓ cup crème fraîche

2¼ cups plain yogurt

1 teaspoon freshly squeezed lemon juice

Salt

Freshly ground black pepper

1 Granny Smith apple, cored and thinly sliced

½ cup walnuts, coarsely chopped

Breadsticks, for serving

Combine the Gorgonzola, cream, crème fraîche, and yogurt in a blender; pulse until smooth and creamy.

Pour into a bowl and season with the lemon juice and salt and pepper to taste. Add the apple slices and chopped walnuts. Serve with breadsticks.

Thick & Spicy BBQ Sauce

Yield: 3 cups sauce   Prep Time: 15 minutes   Cooking Time: 15 minutes

2 cups ketchup

¼ cup cider vinegar

¼ cup Worcestershire sauce

¼ dark brown sugar, firmly packed

2 tablespoons prepared mustard

2 tablespoons molasses

1 tablespoon Tabasco sauce

1 teaspoon sweet paprika

¼ teaspoon coarse salt

1 teaspoon freshly ground black pepper

Pinch of garlic powder

Pinch of onion powder

Pinch of cayenne pepper

½ teaspoon celery seeds

2 teaspoons liquid smoke

In a nonreactive saucepan, combine all the ingredients set over medium-high heat. Slowly bring to a boil, lower the heat, and gently simmer, until the sauce is thick, dark, and flavorful, 10 to 15 minutes.

Transfer the sauce to clean, sterile jars and store in the refrigerator until ready to use. The sauce will keep for several months.

CHAPTER SIX

SALADS & SAVORIES

Potato Salad

Yield: 8 servings   **Prep Time:** 25 minutes   **Cooking Time:** 20 minutes
Chilling Time: 1 hour

2½ pounds Red Bliss potatoes, halved

3 hard-boiled eggs, peeled and diced

4 green onions, finely chopped

2 celery ribs, trimmed and diced

1 red onion, diced

1 tablespoon dried dill

¼ cup sour cream

½ cup mayonnaise

¾ teaspoon dry mustard

1½ tablespoons white distilled vinegar

2 teaspoons sugar

Salt

Freshly ground black pepper

Paprika (optional)

Place the potatoes in a large saucepan and cover with water. Bring to a boil, cover, and simmer over low heat until fork-tender, 15 to 20 minutes. Drain completely and let cool. Roughly cut into bite-size pieces and place in a serving bowl. Add the eggs, green onions, celery, red onion, and dill. Gently toss.

In a small bowl, combine the sour cream, mayonnaise, dry mustard, vinegar, sugar, and salt and pepper to taste. Drizzle the dressing over the potato mixture and toss to coat. Chill in the refrigerator for at least 1 hour prior to serving. Check the seasoning, dust with paprika, if using, and serve.

Greek Salad

Yield: 4 servings   **Prep Time: 20 minutes**

3 ripe tomatoes, sliced into wedges

1 small red onion, sliced into thin strips

1 seedless cucumber, cut into bite-size pieces

1 green bell pepper, trimmed and diced

1 cup fresh flat-leaf parsley, cut into thin strips

⅓ pound feta cheese, crumbled

½ cup pitted kalamata olives

¼ cup good-quality olive oil

3 tablespoons red wine vinegar

½ teaspoon dried oregano

Salt

Freshly ground black pepper

Crusty bread, to serve (optional)

Combine the vegetables, parsley, feta, and olives in a large bowl.

In a small bowl, combine the oil, vinegar, oregano, and salt and black pepper to taste, whisking to blend. Pour the dressing over the salad. Toss well and serve with crusty bread, if desired.

Orzo Salad with Pesto & Chicken

Yield: 8 servings **Prep Time: 25 minutes** **Cooking Time: 8 minutes**

FOR THE PESTO

⅓ cup pine nuts

8 ounces baby spinach, rinsed and stems trimmed

2 garlic cloves, pressed

⅔ cup packed grated Parmesan cheese

1 tablespoon freshly squeezed lemon juice

Salt

Freshly ground black pepper

4 tablespoons good-quality olive oil

FOR THE ORZO SALAD

16 ounces orzo pasta

2 cups cooked chicken breast, cut into bite-size pieces

1 pint cherry tomatoes, halved

2 handfuls baby spinach leaves, rinsed and stems trimmed

1 tablespoon freshly squeezed lemon juice

Salt

Freshly ground black pepper

Prepare the Pesto

In a nonstick skillet, dry roast the pine nuts over medium heat, shaking the skillet back and forth until the pine nuts are golden brown, 1 to 2 minutes. Set aside to cool.

Place the spinach, garlic, toasted pine nuts, Parmesan cheese, and lemon juice in the bowl of a food processor and season with salt and pepper to taste. Drizzle the oil over the top and purée until the mixture is smooth and creamy. Transfer to a large bowl.

Prepare the Orzo Salad

In a pot of salted boiling water, cook the orzo according to the package instructions until al dente, about 8 minutes. Drain well and immediately combine with the pesto, mixing well.

Add the chicken, cherry tomatoes, spinach, and lemon juice. Stir gently to combine. Taste and adjust the salt, pepper, and/or lemon juice as needed. Chill prior to serving.

Grilled Pear & Radicchio Salad

Yield: 4 servings   **Prep Time:** 30 minutes   **Marinating Time:** 2 hours
Grilling Time: 4 minutes

FOR THE PEARS

Leaves from 2 rosemary sprigs, finely chopped

Leaves from 2 thyme sprigs, finely chopped

4 sage leaves, finely chopped

2 garlic cloves, finely chopped

2 tablespoons freshly squeezed lemon juice

1 tablespoon lemon zest

Coarse salt

Freshly ground black pepper

3 tablespoons olive oil

4 firm pears, cored and thickly sliced

FOR THE SALAD

1 tablespoon pine nuts

1 head radicchio, cored

½ cup black olives, pitted and finely chopped

2 parsley sprigs, finely chopped

2 tablespoons freshly squeezed lemon juice

Coarse salt

Freshly ground black pepper

Prepare the Pears

Place the rosemary, thyme, sage, and garlic in a small bowl. Add the lemon juice and zest. Season to taste with salt and pepper; add the olive oil and gently toss.

Arrange the sliced pears in a large bowl or on a baking sheet, drizzle with the marinade, cover, and let stand for 2 hours.

When ready to cook, prepare the grill for direct grilling. Preheat to medium-high heat.

Brush the grill grate lightly with oil. Remove the pears from the marinade (reserving the marinade) and place on the hot grill grate. Grill for 1 to 2 minutes per side, or until golden. Transfer from the hot grill to a serving tray.

Prepare the Salad

Meanwhile, in a large, nonstick skillet over medium heat, dry roast the pine nuts, stirring constantly until they are golden brown, 1 to 2 minutes. Add the radicchio leaves, olives, parsley, and lemon juice and cook for an additional 1 to 2 minutes.

Divide the radicchio mixture evenly among four plates. Top with the grilled pears and drizzle with the reserved marinade. Season with salt and pepper to taste. Serve warm.

Open-Faced Grilled Veggie Antipasto Crostini

Yield: 4 servings　**Prep Time: 30 minutes**　**Grilling Time: 8 minutes**

FOR THE GRILLED VEGETABLE ANTIPASTO

¼ cup good-quality olive oil

2 tablespoons balsamic vinegar

½ bunch fresh basil leaves, divided

1 zucchini, cut lengthwise into ½-inch slices

2 red bell peppers, cored, seeded, and cut into 2-inch strips

8 green onions, tops and bottoms trimmed

Coarse salt

Freshly ground black pepper

FOR THE CROSTINI

2 tablespoons good-quality olive oil

1 tablespoon salted butter, melted

1 garlic clove, crushed

1 tablespoon fresh parsley, finely chopped

Coarse salt

Freshly ground black pepper

4 large slices sourdough or peasant bread

¼ cup balsamic vinegar

1 tablespoon freshly squeezed lemon juice

1 tablespoon fresh basil, finely chopped

Freshly ground black pepper

2 tablespoons olive oil

2 tablespoons safflower oil

TO ASSEMBLE

2 ounces fresh Parmesan cheese, shaved

Coarse salt

Freshly ground black pepper

Prepare the Grilled Vegetable Antipasto

Prepare the grill for direct grilling. Preheat to high heat.

In a small bowl, whisk the olive oil and balsamic vinegar together. Finely chop three or four basil leaves and add to the olive oil mixture, mixing until well blended. Brush the zucchini, bell peppers, and green onions with the oil mixture. When ready to cook, brush the hot grill grate lightly with oil. Place the vegetables on the hot grate and grill for 3 to 4 minutes on each side, or until crisp tender. Season with salt and black pepper to taste. Arrange the grilled vegetables on a serving platter or individual plates.

Prepare the Crostini

In a small bowl, whisk together the olive oil, butter, garlic, parsley, and salt and black pepper to taste until blended. Brush the bread slices lightly with the olive oil mixture and season with salt and black pepper to taste. Toast on the grill until golden brown.

For the Herbed Vinaigrette

In a small bowl, mix together the vinegar, lemon juice, basil, and black pepper to taste. Gradually add the oils, stirring until well blended.

Tip: The vinaigrette can be made ahead; store in an airtight container for up to 1 week.

To Assemble

Arrange the grilled vegetables, remaining fresh basil, and shaved Parmesan on top of the crostini. Season to taste with salt and black pepper. Drizzle with the Herbed Vinaigrette. Serve.

Grilled Baguette with Garlic–Herb Butter

Yield: 4 to 6 servings Prep Time: 5 minutes Grilling Time: 4 minutes

3 tablespoons fresh mixed herbs (parsley, dill, chives, tarragon, basil, cilantro, etc.), finely chopped

2 garlic cloves, pressed

Salt

½ cup (1 stick or 4 ounces) salted butter, at room temperature

1 baguette, cut into ½-inch slices

Prepare the grill for direct grilling. Preheat to medium heat.

In a small bowl, stir the herbs, garlic, and salt to taste into the butter, mixing well to incorporate.

Spread the butter mixture on both sides of the sliced bread and place in a single layer in a long-handled grill basket. Place the grill basket on the hot grill grate and grill for 1 to 2 minutes on each side, or until each side is golden brown. Serve.

CHAPTER SEVEN

SWEET GRILL

Grilled Peaches with Honey–Almond Sauce

Yield: 4 servings   Prep Time: 20 minutes   Grilling Time: 10 minutes

6 ounces flaked almonds

6 tablespoons honey, divided

1 teaspoon pure almond extract

4 ripe peaches

1 lemon

1 cup ricotta cheese

2 tablespoons sugar

Prepare the grill for indirect grilling. Preheat to medium-high heat.

Toast the almond flakes on medium heat in a dry skillet until golden brown. Transfer to a small bowl and combine with 4 tablespoons honey and the almond extract; gently mix. Set aside.

Cut the peaches in half and remove the pits. Oil the grill grate and place the peach halves, cut side down, on the barbecue. Grill for 8 to 10 minutes, until the peaches are soft, watching them carefully.

Meanwhile, rinse the lemon and rub dry; grate the zest. Squeeze 1 tablespoon of juice from the lemon. In a medium bowl, combine the ricotta cheese, sugar, and lemon juice and zest and mix until smooth and creamy.

Spoon half of the ricotta mixture into four serving bowls. Brush each peach half with the remaining 2 tablespoons honey. Place one peach half, cut side up, on top of the ricotta cheese and top with the remaining peach half, followed by a generous spoonful of the remaining ricotta cheese. Spoon the Honey–Almond Sauce over the top and serve immediately.

Caramelized Bananas

Yield: 4 servings   **Prep Time: 10 minutes**   **Cooking Time: 8 minutes**
Grilling Time: 8 minutes

6 tablespoons salted butter

¾ cup light brown sugar

¼ teaspoon salt

1 teaspoon ground cinnamon

1 teaspoon pure vanilla extract

4 ripe bananas

1 cup freshly whipped cream, or 1 pint vanilla ice cream

Prepare the grill for direct grilling. Preheat to medium-high heat.

In a small saucepan, melt the butter over medium heat. Add the brown sugar, salt, and cinnamon. Bring to a boil, stirring to dissolve the sugar. Lower the heat and simmer, stirring frequently, until the mixture thickens, 4 to 5 minutes. Remove from the heat, stir in the vanilla, and set aside.

Peel each banana and cut in half lengthwise. Brush the sliced bananas with the butter mixture. Oil the grill grate and arrange the bananas, cut side down, on the hot grate. Grill until caramelized, 3 to 4 minutes. Carefully turn the bananas and grill until warmed through and caramelized, basting frequently with the butter mixture during the grilling process.

Transfer to a serving platter and serve with a dollop of whipped cream or a scoop of vanilla ice cream. Drizzle with any remaining butter mixture and serve.

Fruit Kebabs with Balsamic Vinegar Syrup

Yield: 4 servings **Prep Time: 30 minutes** **Cooking Time: 5 minutes**
Grilling Time: 5 minutes

2 pears, cored and cut into bite-size chunks

2 apricots, halved and pitted

2 ripe figs, halved

2 ripe mangoes, halved, pitted, and cut into bite-size chunks

2 tablespoons salted butter, melted

2 tablespoons light brown sugar

½ cup balsamic vinegar

Soak 4 to 8 wooden skewers in water for 30 minutes.

Place the prepared fruit in a large bowl. Drizzle the fruit with the melted butter, gently tossing to coat. Sprinkle with the brown sugar, tossing once again to coat. Set aside.

In a small saucepan, simmer the balsamic vinegar over low heat until reduced by half, stirring frequently. Remove from the heat.

Prepare the grill for direct grilling. Preheat to medium heat.

Thread the prepared fruit onto the presoaked wooden skewers. When ready to cook, brush the grill grate lightly with oil. Arrange the skewered fruit on the oiled grill grate. Grill until the sugar caramelizes, 3 to 5 minutes, turning once.

Transfer the fruit from the grill to individual serving plates. Drizzle with the balsamic syrup and serve immediately.

Tip: Other fruit of your choice may be substituted.

Grilled Pineapple

Yield: 4 servings   **Prep Time: 15 minutes**   **Grilling: 8 minutes**

1 ripe pineapple

¼ cup (½ stick) salted butter

4 tablespoons honey

1 tablespoon freshly squeezed lemon juice

1 pinch ground cinnamon

1 pinch ground cloves

⅓ cup warmed gold rum (optional)

Prepare the grill for direct grilling. Preheat to high heat.

Cut the pineapple in half lengthwise, remove the hard core, and cut each half into 4 wedges, for a total of 8 wedges.

In a small saucepan, melt the butter and stir in the honey, lemon juice, and spices.

Grill the pineapple, brushing each wedge with the butter mixture. Turning frequently, grill until evenly browned, about 4 minutes on each side. Do not overcook and watch carefully, as the natural sugars in fresh pineapple caramelize quickly.

Remove the pineapple from the grill and place in a shallow dish. Pour the warmed rum, if using, over the pineapple, flambé, and serve.

Pineapple Upside-Down Cake

Yield: 6 servings   Prep Time: 35 minutes   Grilling Time: 50 minutes

2 cups cake flour

2 teaspoons baking powder

¼ teaspoon salt

¾ cup (1½ sticks or 6 ounces) unsalted butter, at room temperature, divided

1½ cups granulated sugar

3 large eggs, separated

1 cup milk

1 teaspoon pure vanilla extract

1 cup dark brown sugar

1 (20-ounce) can pineapple rings, drained

Prepare the grill for indirect grilling. Preheat to medium heat (about 350°F).

Place a 10-inch cast-iron skillet in the center of the grill and heat thoroughly.

In a medium bowl, sift the cake flour, baking powder, and salt together and set aside. In a large bowl, using an electric mixer, cream together ½ cup of the butter, the granulated sugar, and egg yolks. Lower the mixer speed to low and add the flour mixture to the creamed mixture, alternating with the milk. Beat in the vanilla. In a separate bowl, beat the egg whites until stiff peaks form. Gently fold the egg whites into the batter and set the batter aside.

Place the remaining 4 tablespoons of butter and the brown sugar in the skillet. Allow the mixture to melt and begin to caramelize, then arrange the pineapple rings decoratively in the skillet on top of the caramelized sugar. Pour the batter over the pineapple, filling the skillet to within about ½ inch of the top. Use a rubber spatula to evenly spread the batter.

Bake the cake on the grill with the lid closed, keeping the grill temperature at 350°F, until the top is golden brown and a wooden toothpick inserted into the center of the cake comes out clean, 40 to 50 minutes.

Using ovenproof mitts, remove the skillet from the grill and let the cake cool in the pan for about 10 minutes.

While the cake is still warm, run a butter knife around the edge of the skillet to loosen the cake. Place a serving platter over the top of the skillet and carefully invert the skillet and platter at the same time. Slowly remove the skillet. Serve warm or room temperature.

Cookout S'mores

Yield: 6 servings   Prep Time: 5 minutes   Grilling Time: 3 minutes

12 large marshmallows

3 milk chocolate bars, halved

6 whole graham crackers, halved

Using a long-handled fork, toast the marshmallows over an open flame until golden brown.

Place one chocolate bar half on each of the six graham cracker halves, then top each with two hot toasted marshmallows. Cover with the remaining graham cracker halves and gently squeeze everything together, allowing the toasted marshmallows to melt the chocolate; eat right away.

Grilled Watermelon with Orange Sour Cream Ice Cream

Yield: 4 to 6 servings   **Prep Time: 30 minutes**   **Cooking Time: 21 minutes**
Grilling Time: 4 minutes   **Chilling Time: 3 hours**

FOR THE ORANGE SOUR CREAM ICE CREAM

2 cups half-and-half

1 cup sugar, divided

Grated zest of 2 oranges

1 vanilla bean, split lengthwise

8 large egg yolks

2 cups sour cream

2 teaspoons orange liqueur

FOR THE HONEY–ORANGE SYRUP

Juice of 1 large orange

3 tablespoons honey

2 teaspoons orange liqueur or water

Salt

Freshly ground black pepper

¼ whole watermelon, sliced, rind removed, cut into 1-inch-thick triangles

Honey, for brushing watermelon

Fresh mint, for garnish

Prepare the Orange Sour Cream Ice Cream:

In a heavy-bottomed saucepan, combine the half-and-half, ¾ cup of the sugar, orange zest, and split vanilla bean; bring just to the boiling point. Remove the saucepan from the heat.

In a large bowl, whisk the egg yolks and remaining ¼ cup of sugar together. Pour in the hot half-and-half mixture gradually, whisking to incorporate. Transfer the blended egg mixture to the saucepan and cook over low heat, stirring continuously, until it reaches 170°F on a candy thermometer.

Once again, remove the pan from the heat. Scrape the seeds from the vanilla bean into the mixture and discard the pod. Mix in the sour cream and orange liqueur, stirring until well combined. Chill the custard in the refrigerator for several hours, until cold.

Process the custard in an ice-cream maker according to the manufacturer's instructions. Store in an airtight container in the freezer until ready to serve.

Prepare the Honey–Orange Syrup:

In a small bowl, combine all the ingredients, stirring to blend well. Set aside.

Prepare the Grilled Watermelon:

Preheat the grill or a grill pan to high heat. Brush both sides of the cut watermelon with honey. Grill until just browned, 1 to 2 minutes per side. Transfer the watermelon to serving plates. Drizzle with the Honey–Orange Syrup and garnish with fresh mint. Serve with the ice cream.

Index

*Italics indicate illustrations.